CANADA+TATTOO
Coloring book for Adults Relaxation Meditation Blessing

Tanna G. Tepper

CANADA+TATTOO
Coloring book for Adults Relaxation Meditation Blessing

Copyright: Published in the United States by **Tanna G. Tepper**

All rights reserved. No part of this publication may be reproduced, stored in retrieval system, copied in any form or by any means, electronic, mechanical, photocopying, recording or otherwise transmitted without written permission from the publisher. Please do not participate in or encourage piracy of this material in any way. You must not circulate this book in any format. Tanna G. Tepper *does not control or direct users' actions and is not responsible for the information or content shared, harm and/or actions of the book readers.*

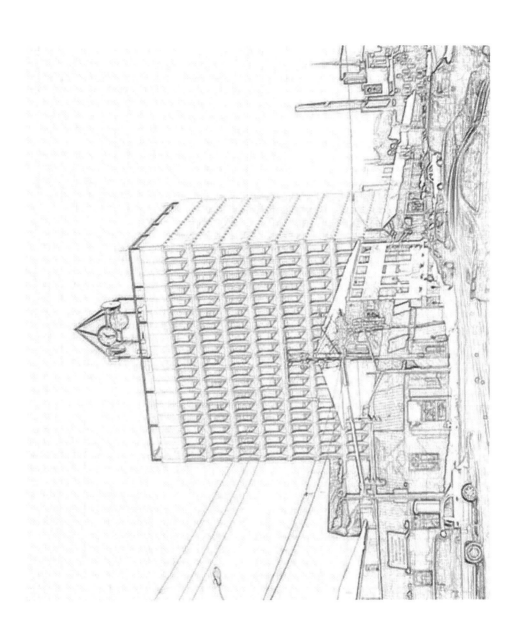

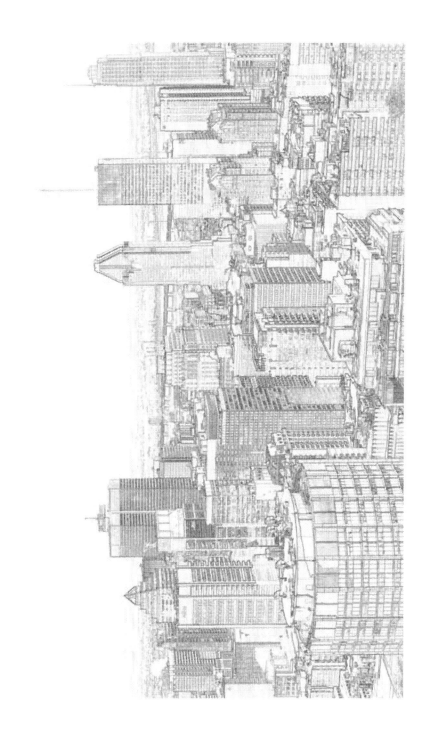

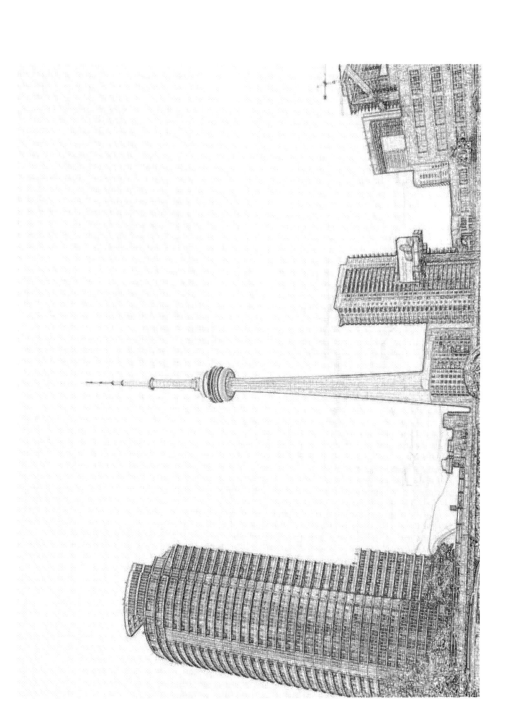

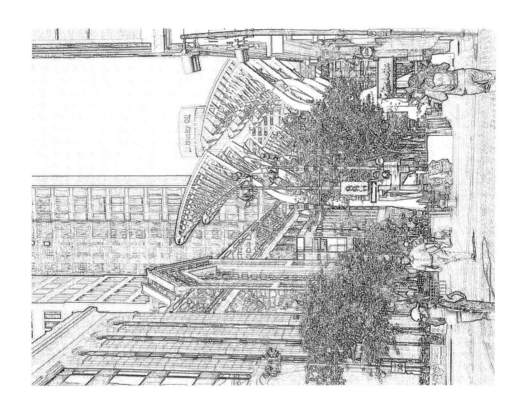

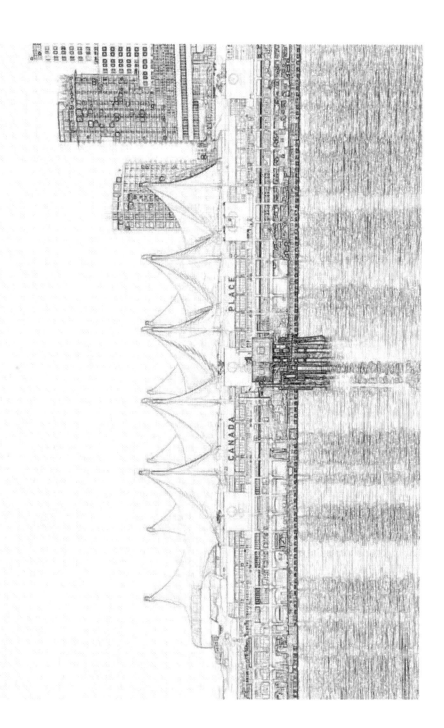

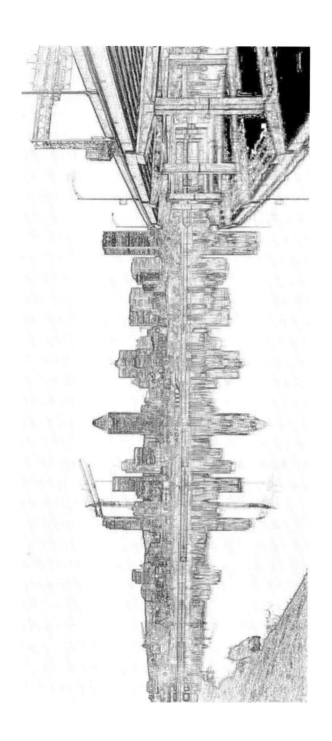

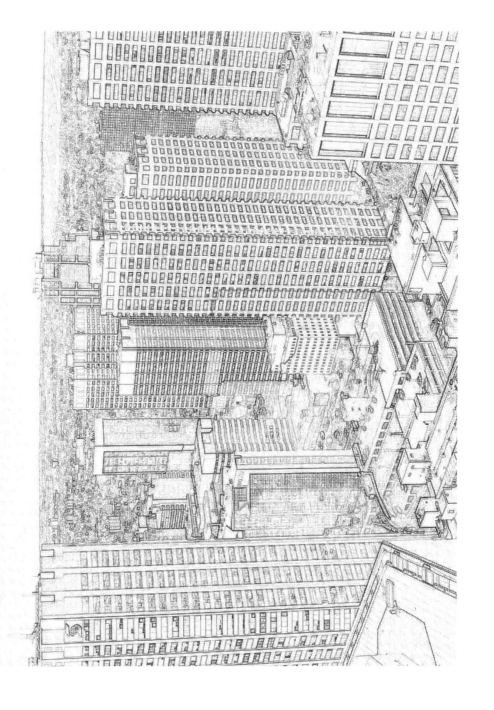

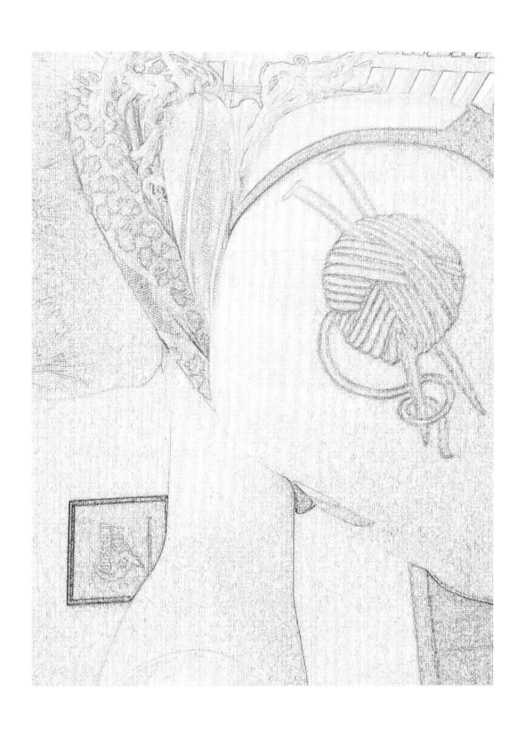

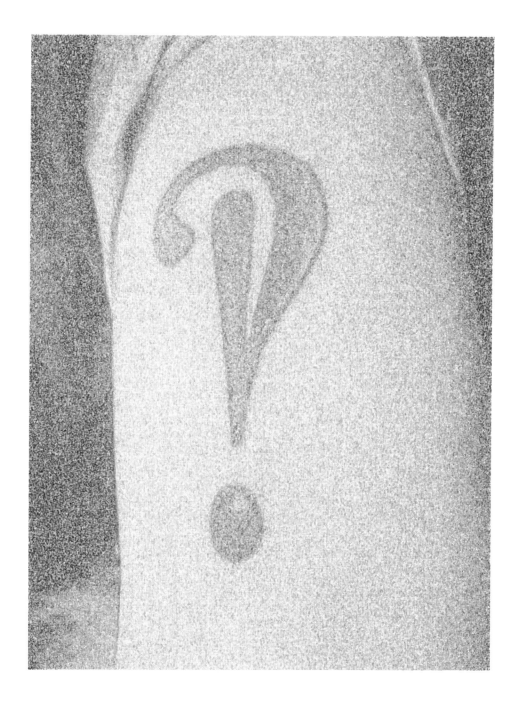

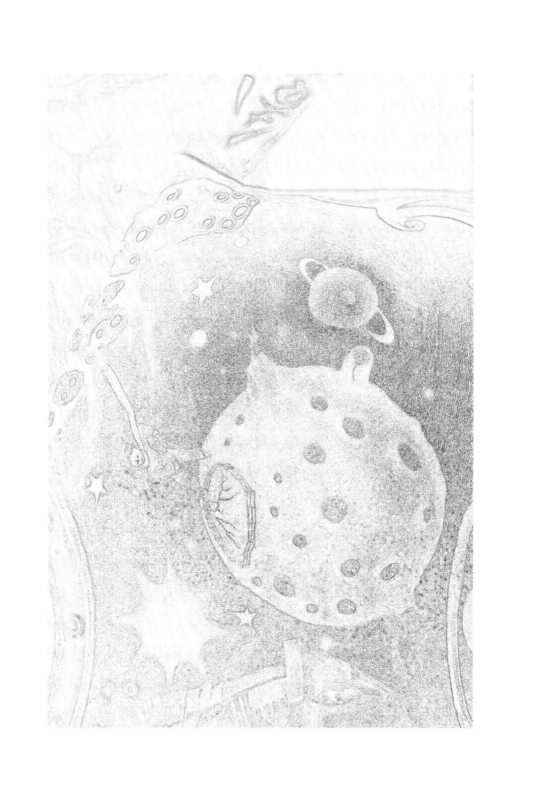

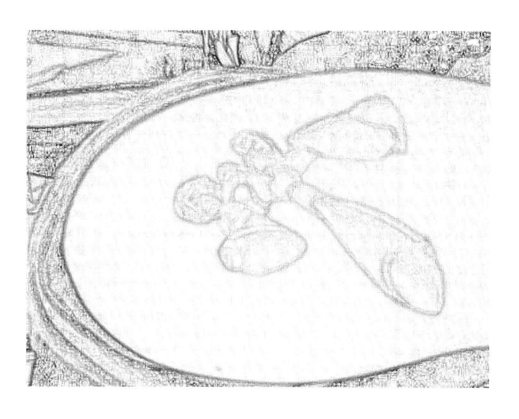

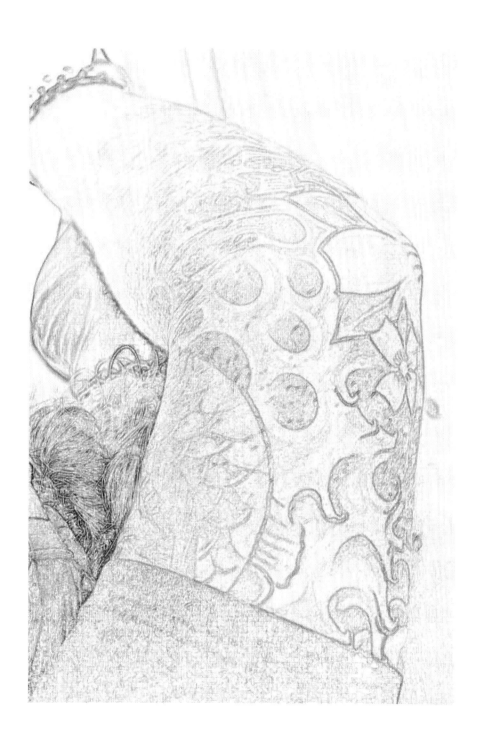

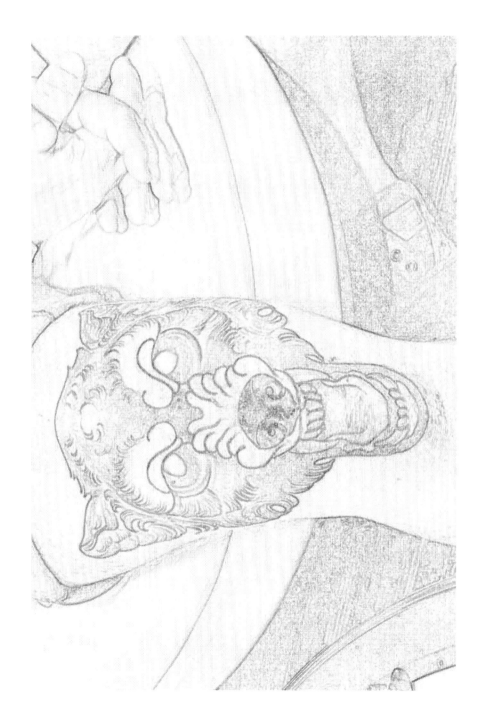

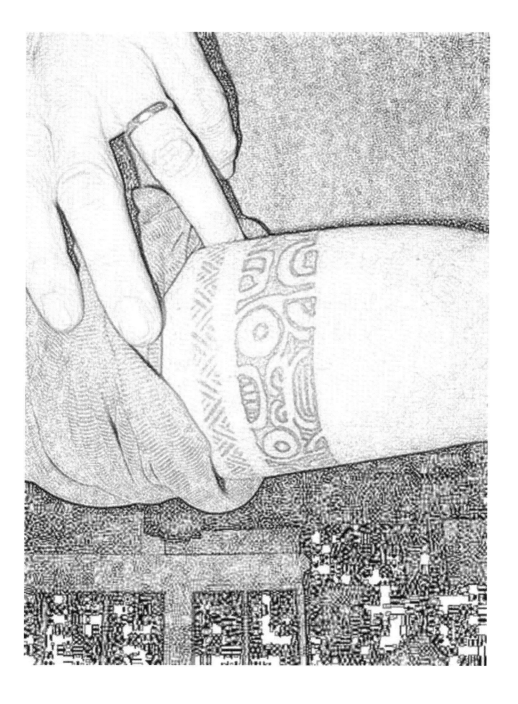

Thank you

Made in the USA
Monee, IL
24 February 2021